THE JOY OF
POPULAR
CHRISTMAS SONGS

Arranged by David Pearl.

YORKTOWN MUSIC PRESS
New York/London/Paris/Sydney/Copenhagen/Berlin/Tokyo/Madrid

Cover design and art direction by Michael Bell Design.
Cover illustration by Andrew Selby.
Arranged for publication by David Pearl.

Order No. YK22011
International Standard Book Number: 978-0-8256-8114-1
HL Item Number: 14037676

Exclusive Distributor for the United States, Canada, Mexico and US possessions:
Hal Leonard Corporation
7777 West Bluemound Road, Milwaukee, WI 53213 USA.

Exclusive Distributors for the rest of the World:
Music Sales Limited
14-15 Berners Street, London W1T 3LJ, UK.
Music Sales Pty Limited
20 Resolution Drive, Caringbah, NSW 2229, Australia.

Printed in the United States of America by
Vicks Lithograph and Printing Corporation.

Blue Christmas

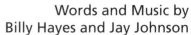

Words and Music by
Billy Hayes and Jay Johnson

Slowly

I'll have a   blue   Christ-mas with-out you. _____   I'll be so

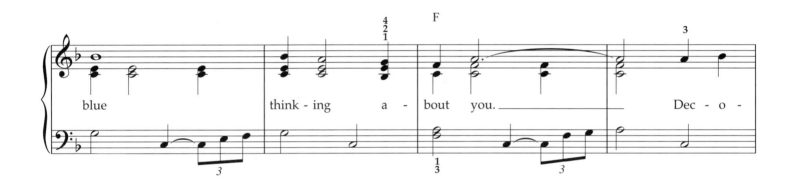

blue   think-ing a-bout you. _____   Dec-o-

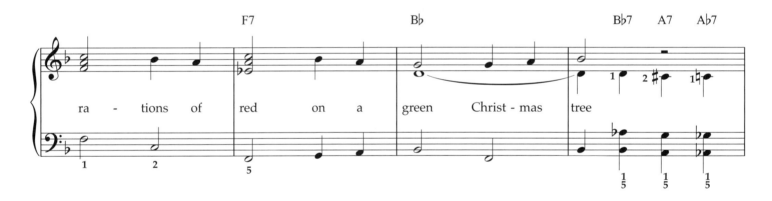

ra- tions of   red   on a   green   Christ-mas   tree

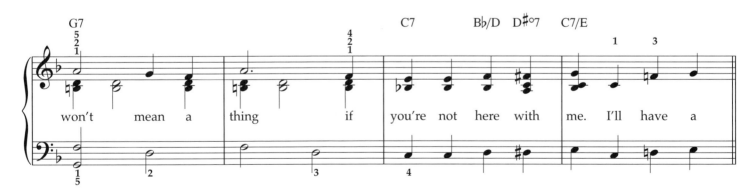

won't   mean a   thing   if   you're not   here with   me. I'll have a

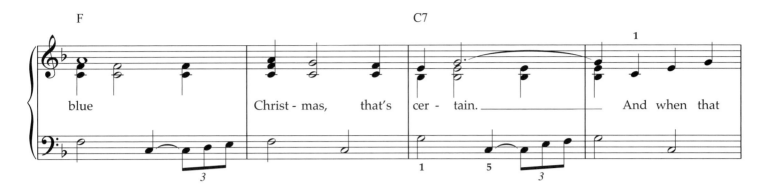

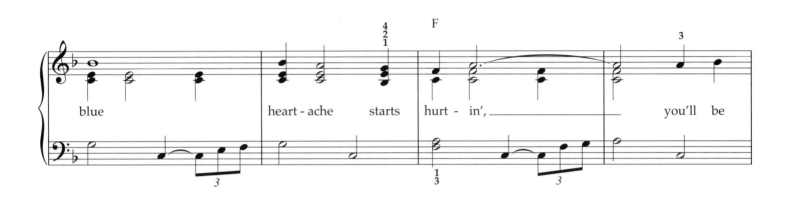

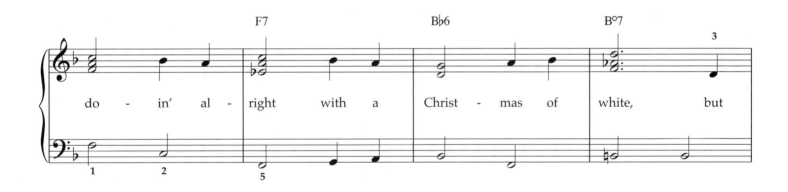

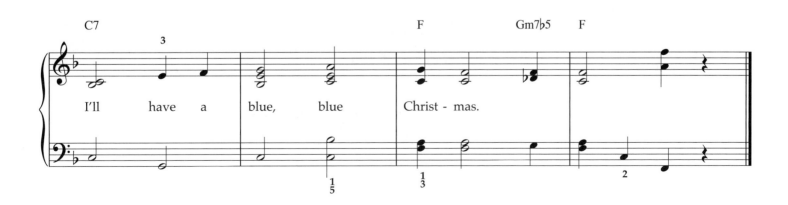

I Heard The Bells On Christmas Day

Music by Johnny Marks
Lyrics by Henry Wadsworth Longfellow
Adapted by Johnny Marks

Slowly, in 2

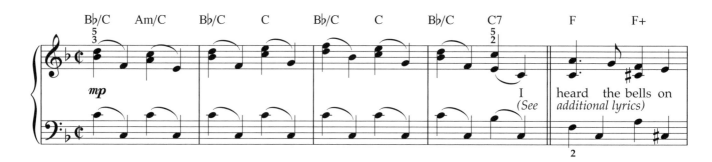

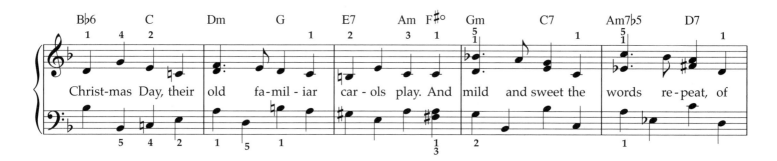

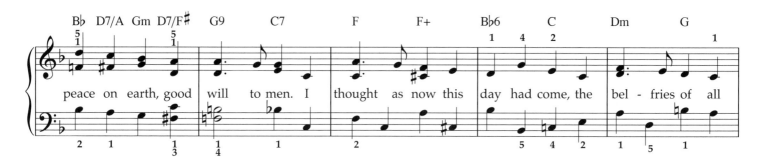

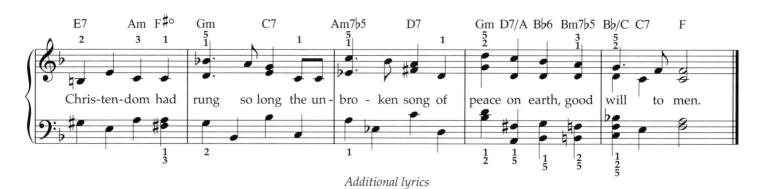

Additional lyrics

2. And in despair, I bowed my head,
   "There is no peace on Earth," I said,
   "For hate is strong and mocks the song
   Of peace on earth, good will to men."
   Then pealed the bells more loud and deep,
   "God is not dead, nor doth He sleep,
   The wrong shall fail, the right prevail,
   With peace on earth, good will to men."

C-H-R-I-S-T-M-A-S

Words by Jenny Lou Carson
Music by Eddy Arnold

Moderately

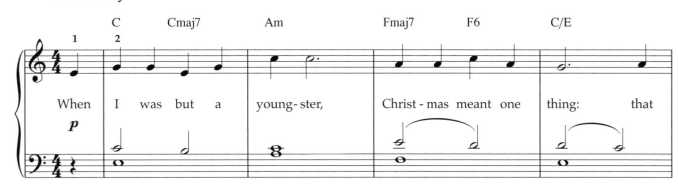

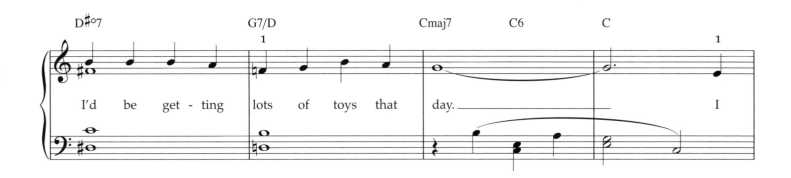

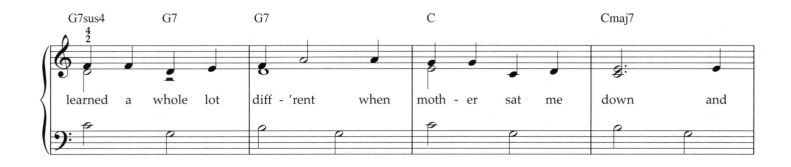

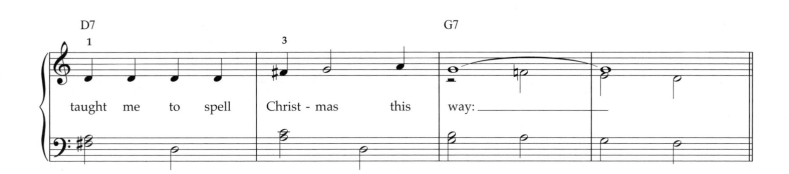

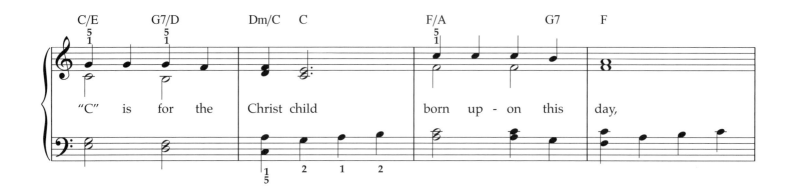

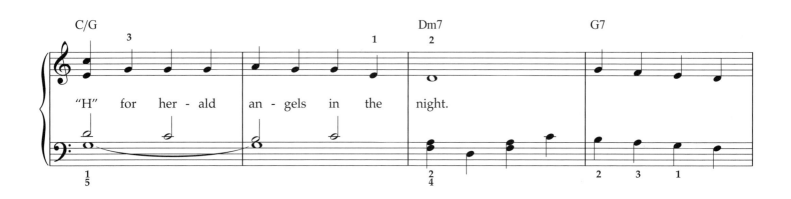

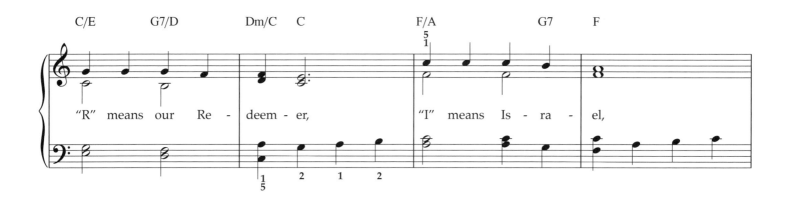

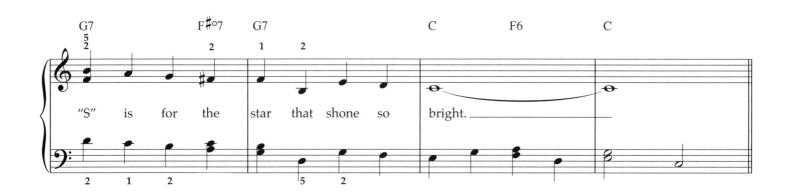

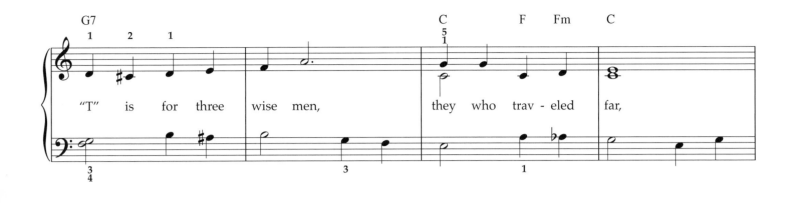

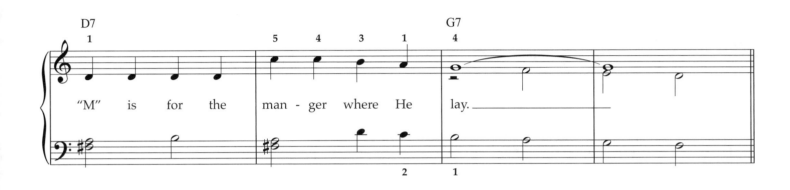

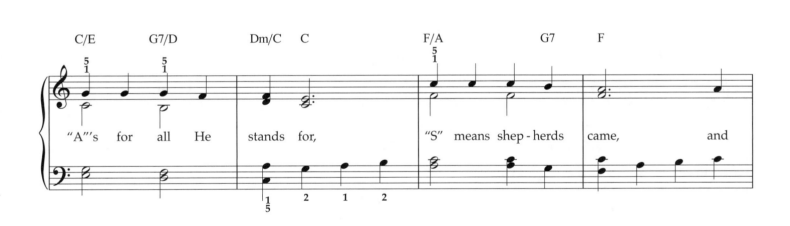

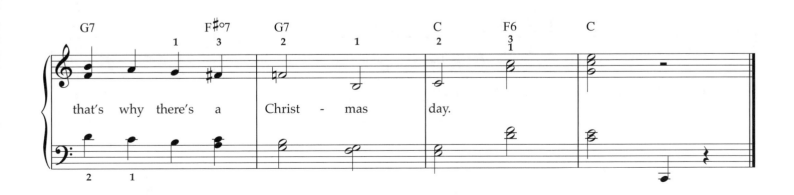

9

The Christmas Waltz

Words by Sammy Cahn
Music by Jule Styne

Bright Waltz

Do They Know It's Christmas?

Words and Music by
M. Ure and B. Geldof

Moderately

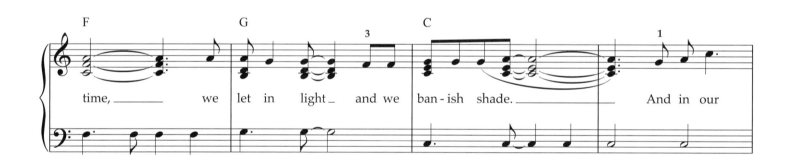

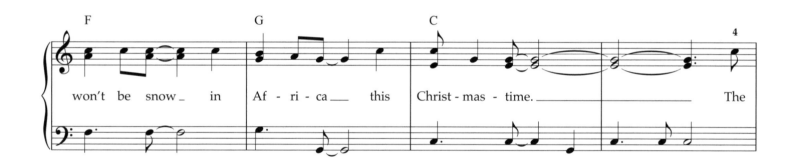

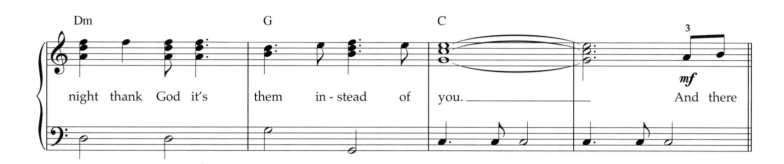

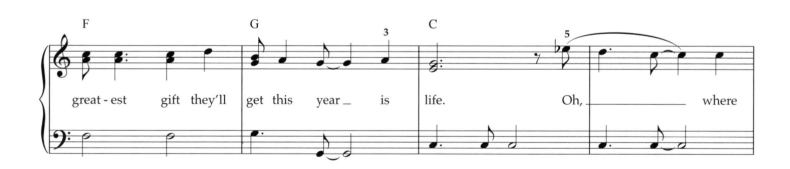

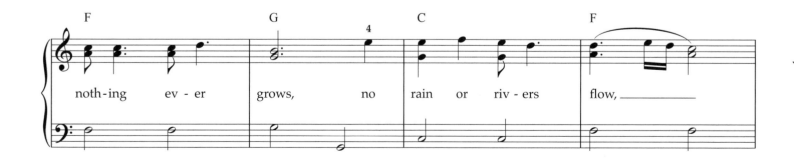

Frosty The Snow Man

Words and Music by
Steve Nelson and Jack Rollins

Additional lyrics

2. Frosty the snowman knew the sun was hot that day,
But he said, "Let's run and we'll have some fun now, before I melt away."
Down to the village with a broomstick in his hand,
Running here and there, all around the square, sayin', "Catch me if you can."
He led them down the streets of town, right to the traffic cop,
And he only paused a moment when he heard them holler, "Stop!"
For Frosty the snowman had to hurry on his way,
But he waved goodbye, saying, "Don't you cry, I'll be back again someday."

The Greatest Gift Of All

Words and Music by
John Jarvis

Grown-Up Christmas List

Words and Music by
David Foster and Linda Thompson-Jenner

Additional lyrics

2. As children we believed the grandest sight to see
Was something lovely wrapped beneath our tree.
Well, heaven surely knows that packages and bows
Can never heal a hurting human soul.

(There's No Place Like)
Home For The Holidays

Al Stillman and Robert Allen

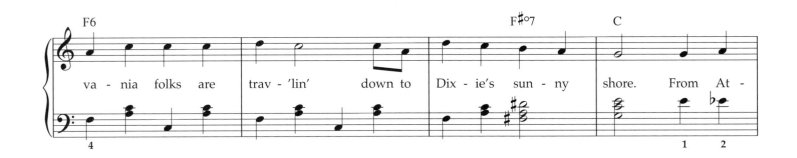

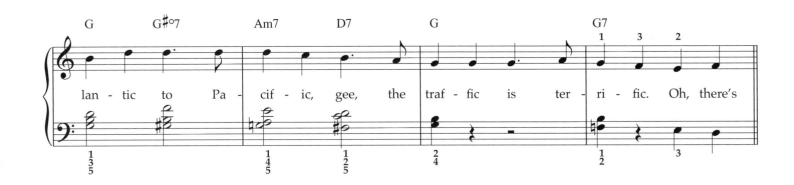

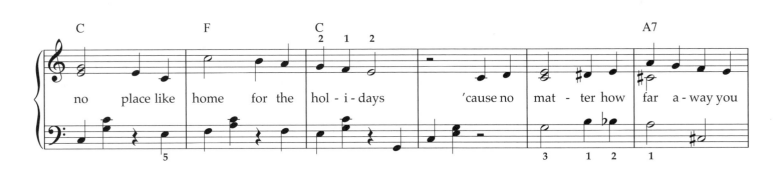

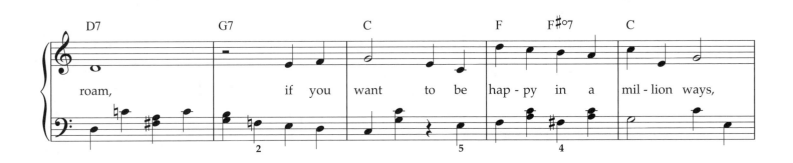

Jingle-Bell Rock

Words and Music by
Joe Beal and Jim Boothe

Moderate Swing

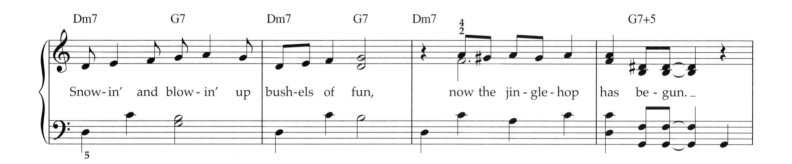

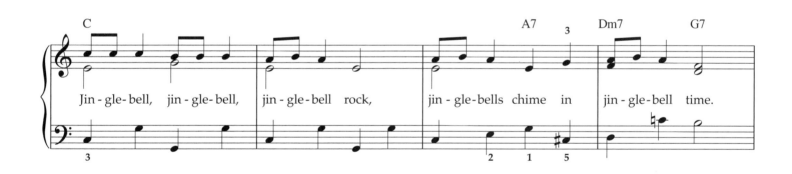

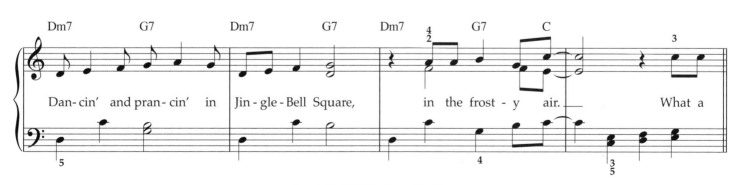

Let It Snow! Let It Snow! Let It Snow!

Words by Sammy Cahn
Music by Jule Styne

Little Saint Nick

Words and Music by
Brian Wilson and Mike Love

32

Merry Christmas, Darling

Words and Music by
Richard Carpenter and Frank Pooler

March Of The Toys

Victor Herbert

Bright March

Mistletoe And Holly

Words and Music by
Frank Sinatra, Dok Stanford and Henry W. Sanicola

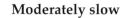

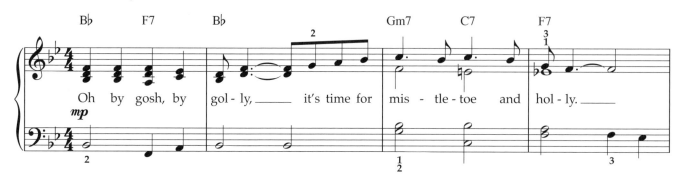

Oh by gosh, by gol - ly, _____ it's time for mis - tle - toe and hol - ly. _____

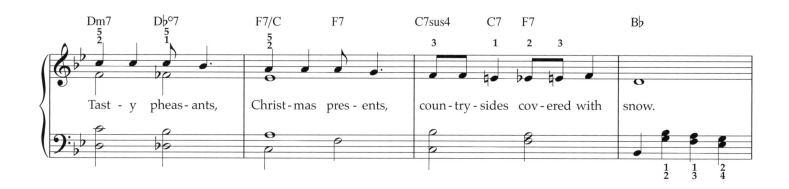

Tast - y pheas - ants, Christ - mas pres - ents, coun - try - sides cov - ered with snow.

Oh by gosh, by jin - gle, _____ it's time for car - ols and Kris Krin - gle. _____

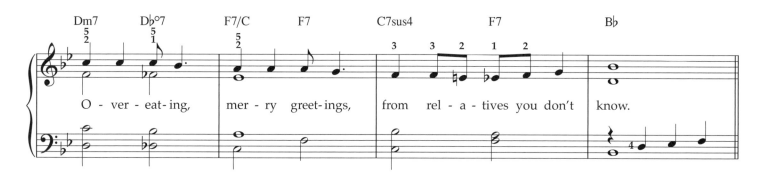

O - ver - eat - ing, mer - ry greet - ings, from rel - a - tives you don't know.

The Most Wonderful Time Of The Year

Eddie Pola and George Wyle

Bright Waltz

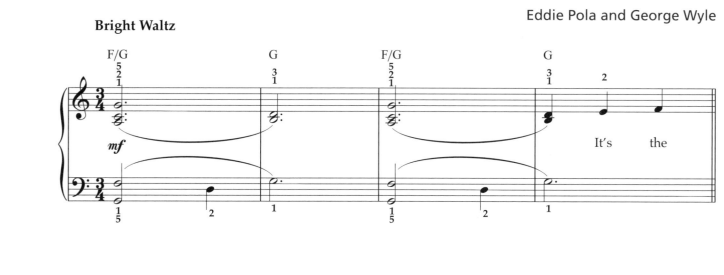

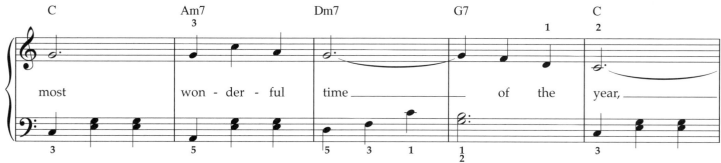

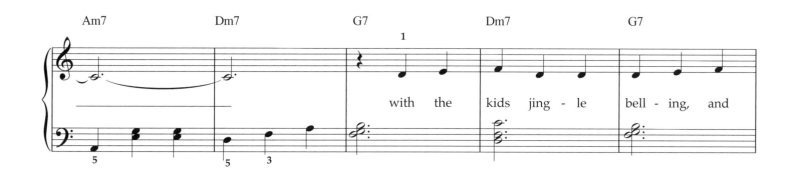

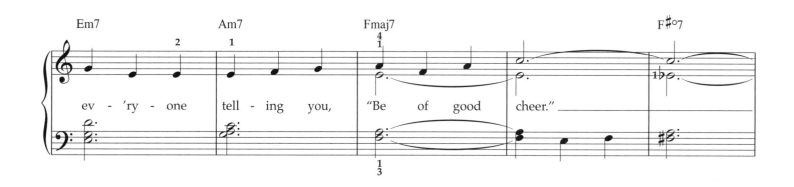

Nuttin' For Christmas

Words and Music by
Roy Bennett and Sid Tepper

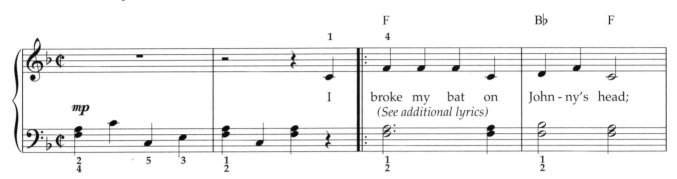

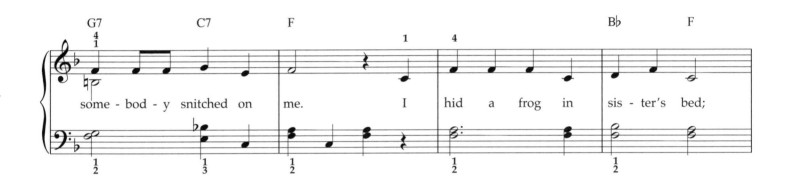

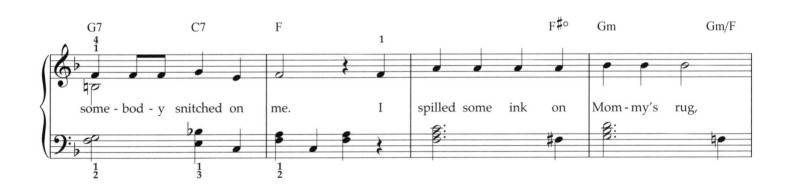

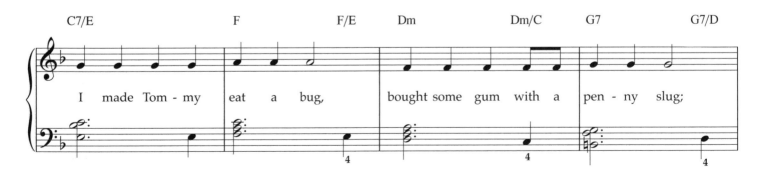

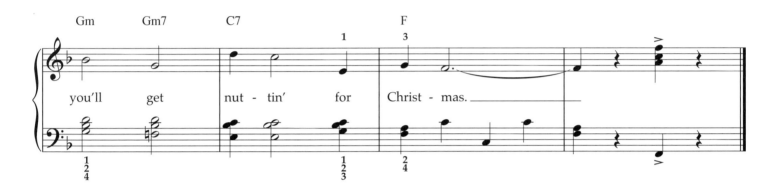

Additional lyrics

2. I put a tack on teacher's chair;
   Somebody snitched on me.
   I tied a knot in Susie's hair;
   Somebody snitched on me.
   I did a dance on Mommy's plants,
   Climbed a tree and tore my pants,
   Filled the sugar bowl with ants;
   Somebody snitched on me. So,...

3. I won't be seeing Santa Claus;
   Somebody snitched on me.
   He won't come visit me because
   Somebody snitched on me.
   Next year I'll be going straight,
   Next year I'll be good, just wait,
   I'd start now but it's too late;
   Somebody snitched on me. So,...

This One's For The Children

Words and Music by
Maurice Starr

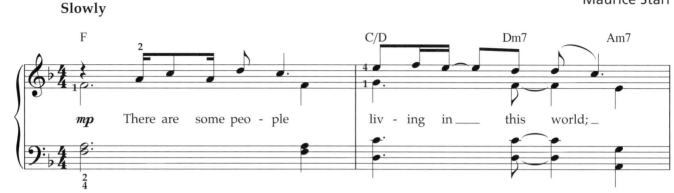

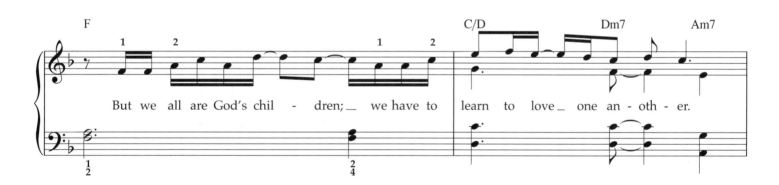

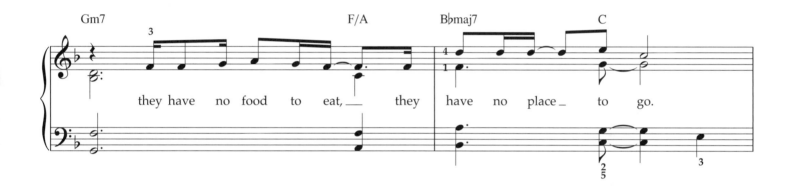

51

An Old Fashioned Christmas

Music and Lyrics by
Johnny Marks

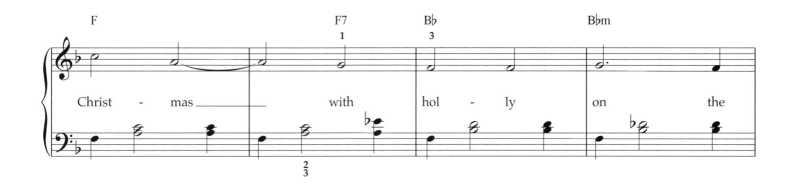

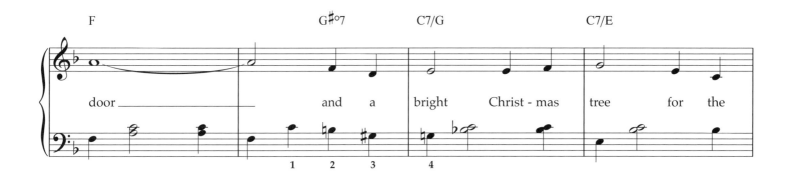

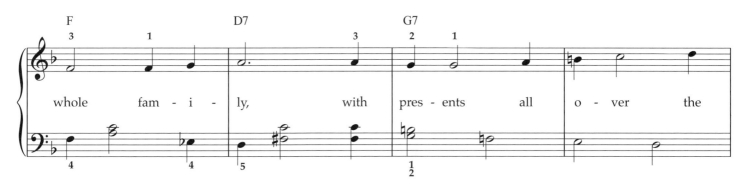

53

Parade Of The Wooden Soldiers

Leon Jessel and Ballard MacDonald

Moderate March

Rockin' Around The Christmas Tree

Music and Lyrics by
Johnny Marks

Shake Me I Rattle (Squeeze Me I Cry)

Words and Music by
Hal Hackady and Charles Naylor

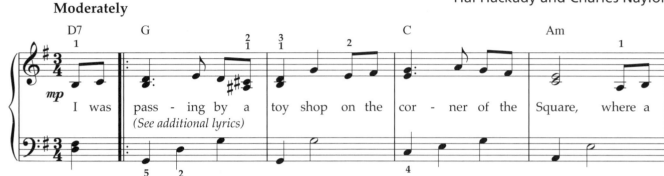

I was pass - ing by a toy shop on the cor - ner of the Square, where a
(See additional lyrics)

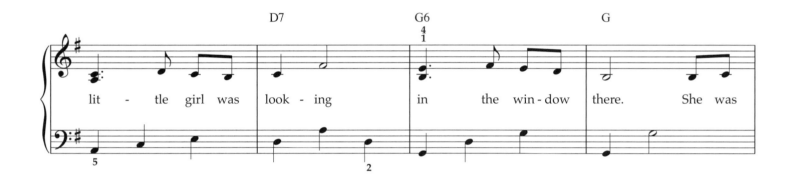

lit - tle girl was look - ing in the win - dow there. She was

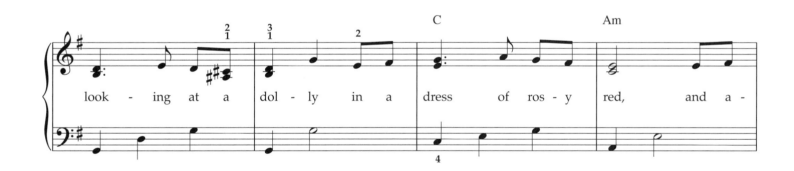

look - ing at a dol - ly in a dress of ros - y red, and a -

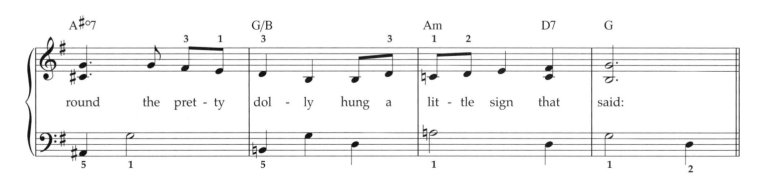

round the pret - ty dol - ly hung a lit - tle sign that said:

Additional lyrics

2. I recalled another toy shop on a square so long ago,
   Where I saw a little dolly that I wanted so.
   I remembered, I remembered how I longed to make it mine,
   And around that other dolly hung another little sign:
   Shake me, I rattle, Squeeze me, I cry.
   I had counted my pennies, just a penny shy.
   Shake me, I rattle, Squeeze me, I cry.
   Please take me home and love me.

3. It was late and snow was falling as the shoppers hurried by
   Past the girlie at the window with her little head held high.
   They were closing up the toy shop as I hurried through the door
   Just in time to buy the dolly that her heart was longing for:
   Shake me, I rattle, Squeeze me, I cry.
   And I gave her the dolly that we both had longed to buy.
   Shake me, I rattle, Squeeze me, I cry.
   Please take me home and love me.

Snowfall

Lyrics by Ruth Thornhill
Music by Claude Thornhill

Suzy Snowflake

Words and Music by
Sid Tepper and Roy Bennett

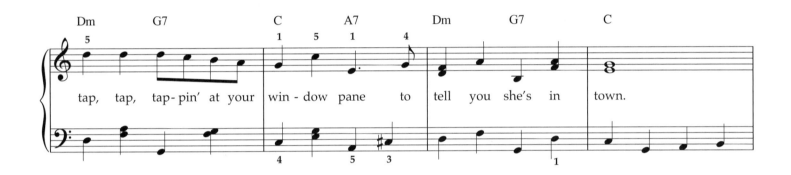

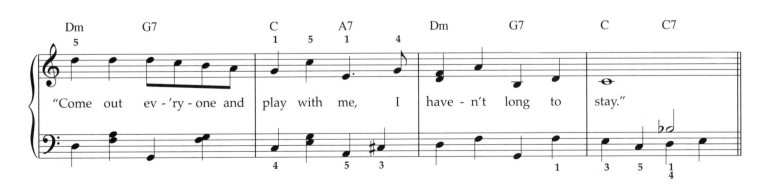

Toyland

Victor Herbert and Glen MacDonough

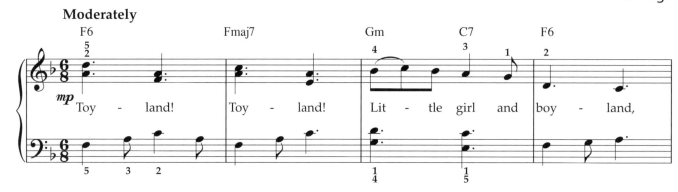

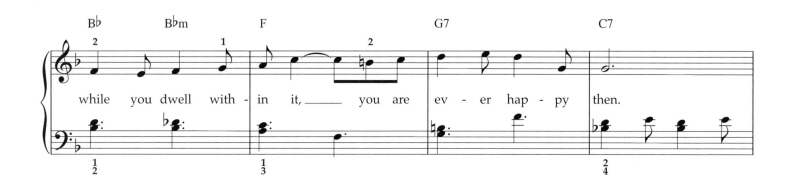

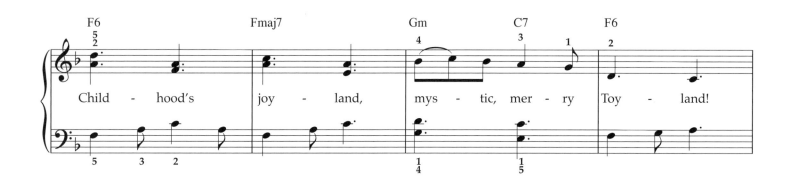

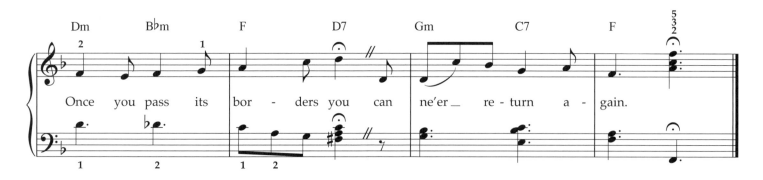